CREATIVE MICROWAVE COOKBOOK

Irena Chalmers
Richard Ahrens and Ruth Malinowski

Bonanza Books
New York

PICTURE CREDITS

The following pictures were provided through the
courtesy of Transworld Feature Syndicate, Inc.:

Syndication International: pp. 12   15   17   19   20
23   24   25   27   28   29   31   39   47   50   54   56
57   58   59

Lennart Osbeck: pp. 34   43   45   52
Scoop: pp. 30   36   42
Michael Holtz: p. 41

1985 edition published by Bonanza Books,
distributed by Crown Publishers, Inc.
ISBN: 0-517-60581-3
Published under arrangement with Ottenheimer Publishers, Inc.
Printed in Brazil
h g f e d c b a

Contents

Preface   6

Introduction   7

Appetizers and Soups   12

Meats   21

Poultry   33

Seafood   40

Vegetables   49

Desserts   55

Index   61

preface

The microwave oven has recently moved from the heady realms of luxury into the area of practical necessity. It is now possible to prepare a meal in only a fraction of the time needed to cook by more traditional methods. The manufacturers have improved the performance of the oven to the point that it is not only conceivable but very likely that it may soon supplement or replace the conventional range completely. Already microwave ovens are seen as an essential appliance for every modern kitchen.

The microwave oven eliminates the necessity to plan meals ahead. Even long-cooking foods are ready in minutes rather than hours. Foods can be taken directly from the freezer and defrosted in a very short period of time. With a well-stocked freezer there is always something good to eat both for the family and for unexpected guests. Late arrivals can have a plate of appetizing hot food ready to eat in seconds. The meal will have all the qualities of freshly cooked food, for one of the great advantages of cooking in the microwave oven is that reheated food does not become dry, as is often the case with foods reheated in the conventional oven or on top of the range. Instead the colors remain bright and clear, the food is moist and tasty, and more of the nutrients are retained because the cooking time is so brief.

The microwave oven uses less energy to cook food than does the conventional oven. The microwave oven does not need to be preheated, but instead the cooking starts the moment the door is closed. There are few spills, and the oven needs only a quick flip of a sponge to become spotlessly clean. As all the cooking is done in glass, china, or ceramic utensils or with paper products, the clean-up chores are finished very quickly.

The oven is useful not only for the preparation of entire meals but for speeding separate steps in the cooking; for melting butter and chocolate, for heating liquids, for drying bread crumbs, for toasting nuts, and for a thousand other time-consuming processes.

Having a microwave oven in the kitchen is like having two extra pairs of hands working for you, and, though nothing makes cooking entirely effortless, the microwave oven makes everything faster and easier.

introduction

How Does It Work?

Imagine you are walking beside a still, quiet pond. It is a windless day and the surface of the water is calm and smooth. If you throw a stone into the pond, it will sink, and ripples or waves will be produced in ever-widening circles radiating from the point at which the stone entered the water. The circles of waves that are generated will be of different sizes; the inner, shorter waves will travel faster and with greater energy than the outer waves.

Electromagnetic waves are short waves that travel at the speed of light, 186,000 miles per second. These waves carry photons that vibrate to produce energy. The number or frequency of the vibrations determines the amount of energy produced.

In a microwave oven the microwaves are produced by a magnetron. This is the equivalent of throwing a stone in a pond. The microwaves are produced the moment the oven door is closed by the conversion of electricity to electromagnetic energy. When the microwaves enter the oven, they are interrupted by a stirrer that scatters and distributes them evenly throughout the interior of the oven. The microwaves then enter the food, and the vibration of the waves produces heat energy that is absorbed from the outside to the center of the food. It is the intramolecular friction that produces the heat to cook the food. The higher the moisture content of the food, the faster it will cook. Microwaves cause the moisture cells within the food to vibrate at approximately two and a half million times a second. This is why microwave cooking is so much faster than conventional conduction cooking.

Understanding The Microwave Oven

If you heat a cup of water in a saucepan on top of the stove, it will reach the boiling point more rapidly over high heat than if you put it on a low flame.

If you heat a cup of water in the microwave oven, it will take roughly 2 minutes to reach the boiling point. There is no equivalent of a high flame in the microwave oven. It takes all the available microwave energy to make this quantity of water boil. Therefore, if it takes 2 minutes for 1 cup of water to boil, it will take more energy,—that is, more time—for 2 cups of water to reach the boiling point.

If you put a cup of hot water in the microwave oven, it will reach the boiling point more rapidly than a cup of iced water. If you defrost food taken from a freezer at 0 degrees, it will take longer to defrost than food from the freezer above the refrigerator. A refrigerator freezer cannot maintain as low a temperature as a separate freezer.

If you bake 1 potato in the conventional oven at 350° F, it will take 1 hour to cook. It will take the same length of time if you bake 2 or 6 potatoes simultaneously. This is because all the potatoes are equally surrounded by a mass of hot air. If you lower the temperature, the potatoes will take longer to cook. If you increase the temperature, they will cook more rapidly.

However, if you put 1 potato in the microwave oven, it will be baked in 4 minutes. All the available microwave energy is used in cooking the single potato. The air in the microwave oven remains at room temperature. It therefore takes a longer time to cook 2 or more potatoes.

If you reheat bread, it will be hot faster than if you reheat a pork chop. Bread is more porous than meat.

If you cook an unevenly shaped food, such as a leg of lamb, in the microwave oven, it will cook in the same way as in the conventional oven to the extent that the thinner parts will cook more quickly than the thicker parts. To cook food evenly, thinner parts can be protected by wrapping them in lightweight aluminum foil halfway through the cooking period.

Although the "heat" cannot be increased in the microwave oven, the amount of energy reaching the food can be decreased. Every oven manufacturer uses different but similar terminology in differentiating between the highest setting, roast and simmer settings and the slower speed of the defrost setting, but they all follow the same patterns. Do be sure to read the written material that accompanies every new microwave oven, because, in order to get the maximum satisfaction from the oven, you must understand the way it works.

Though all these facts are obvious, and I hesitate to mention them, they are, surprisingly, not nearly as apparent when you first start cooking with microwave energy. You may at first be quite impatient with the oven, but after a very short time and with the help of a little experience you will soon not only become used to it but quite dependent on it, too. At this point you will be able to adapt your favorite recipes for the oven and save hours of cooking time.

Assessing the Microwave Oven

All scientific, industrial, medical, and cooking equipment that uses shortwave energy is permitted to operate only if it conforms with the strict and rigidly enforced standards of safety established by the Federal Communications Commission. In spite of rumors to the contrary a microwave oven that is not in use is no more hazardous than a television set or a radio that is turned off. Both television sets and radios are powered by microwave energy. There is, furthermore, no possibility of leakage of microwaves when the oven is in actual use. This is because every microwave oven is equipped with a fail-safe mechanism that automatically causes the oven to shut itself off if any part is not functioning correctly.

The unreasoning fear of cooking in a microwave oven has, in the past, been a significant factor in the slow public acceptance of this method of preparing food. Yet this attitude is based on emotion rather than fact. Dread warnings have almost always circulated around new inventions (if man had been meant to fly, he would have been given wings, etc.). Throughout history the stalwart defenders of the status quo have denounced everything from the electric light bulb to the automobile, but the time interval between the proposal of a new idea and its acceptance by the mass market is becoming shorter and shorter, and it will not be many years before the microwave oven is a standard part of every new kitchen.

Why Metal Must Not Be Used in the Microwave Oven

The walls of the microwave oven are made of metal. Metal reflects microwaves like a mirror to bounce the energy into the cavity of the oven. If a metal pan or any other metal object is placed in the oven, the energy bounces off the oven walls to the object, back to the walls, and back again to the object. This causes an effect known as "arcing" and is immediately and dramatically apparent in the form of a series of intensely bright light flashes. This arcing effect will continue until the oven is turned off.

Objects as small as a metal skewer, a meat thermometer, or even the presence of metal in the painted designs on plates will cause arcing. It not only slows down or prevents the cooking of the food, but it can also cause serious and irreversible damage to the magnetron that converts electricity to microwave energy.

A lightweight piece of aluminum foil does not cause arcing as long as the foil is not actually touching the walls of the oven, but the heavier weight of a ¾-inch-deep aluminum tray, containing, for example, a TV dinner, cannot be used. The food must be transferred to a plate. If you are in any doubt about a utensil, fill it with a cup of water. If the utensil becomes hot within 2 minutes, do not use it.

Cooking Utensils for the Microwave Oven

Microwaves pass unhindered through glass, ceramics, china, and certain other materials as though they were not there, in a similar way to sunlight passing unobstructed through a window. The sun heats the room while the window remains at the same temperature as the air surrounding it. This is why utensils used in the microwave oven remain cool to the touch even when the food is boiling hot, though sometimes there can be transference of heat from the food to the cooking utensil after a long cooking time.

Glass, ceramics, china, paper, and some plastics can all be used in the oven, both for cooking and for reheating the food. Wax-treated paper can be used, but transparent wraps may melt in the microwave oven.

Pottery and earthenware bowls are suitable for use in the oven if they do not contain any traces of lead or other metal. Clay pots can also be used.

Frozen vegetables can be reheated in their cardboard boxes if one end is opened to allow the steam to escape.

Plastic cooking pouches can be used, but cut a slit in the pouch to allow the steam to escape. Duck can be defrosted in its plastic wrapping, but again be sure to cut a slit for steam to escape.

"Take out" foods can be reheated in the carrying containers unless the boxes are sealed with metal staples.

Advantages of Cooking in a Microwave Oven

SPEED

A simple meal for one or two people can be prepared in one-quarter to one-fifth of the conventional cooking time. (Larger quantities of food require longer cooking times.)

CONVENIENCE

Frozen foods can be defrosted in a fraction of the conventional time. Foods prepared in advance need only seconds to reheat and look and taste as appetizing as when they were first made.

CLEAN COOKING

The oven is very quick and easily cleaned. The cooking utensils can all be put into a dishwasher, and paper products used for cooking are thrown away.

COOL COOKING

The kitchen does not become hot because the food is cooked by internal friction and the heat remains confined to the food itself.

BABY FOODS

Baby foods and bottles can be warmed in their own containers, with the metal lids removed. A jar of junior food is warmed in 30 seconds.

Quick-Cooking Techniques

The total length of time spent in the preparation of many foods can be considerably reduced by the use of the microwave oven. The oven is used on the highest setting for all the following preparations.

To soften butter, place the butter in a small bowl—2 tablespoons of butter are softened in 15 seconds; 2 tablespoons of butter are sizzling hot in 40 seconds.

To melt chocolate, put it on a plate and soften 6 ounces of semisweet chocolate pieces in 1 minute, without added water.

To toast nuts and bread crumbs, spread them on a plate and cook a 1-cup quantity for 3 minutes, stirring every minute.

To heat maple syrup for pancakes, remove the lid from the container and cook for 30 seconds. (Sugar heats very quickly in the microwave oven.)

To speed the defrosting of frozen juices, remove the metal cap from the container and heat for 1 minute. (The metal base will not cause the arcing effect usually seen when metal is used in the microwave oven.)

To prepare hot drinks, fill a cup with the liquid and heat for 2 minutes.

To peel tomatoes, peaches, and other soft foods, heat them for 30 seconds and let stand for 2 minutes. If the fruit is underripe, heat for 10 seconds longer.

To obtain more juice from lemons and other citrus fruits, heat for 30 seconds. This technique can also be used before processing vegetable juices in a juice extractor.

To soften dried fruits, place 1 cup of raisins, prunes, apples, or apricots in a bowl. Cover with water and heat for 5 minutes.

To caramelize sugar for making caramel custard or butterscotch sauce, place ½ cup sugar in a bowl and cook for 3 minutes, until a golden brown liquid is formed.

To speed the preparation time of foods cooked on an outdoor grill, precook the food for half the estimated cooking time in the microwave oven. Finish the cooking on the grill outside. Precooking prevents the outside of the food from becoming charred while the inside is still raw.

To heat a sandwich filling, place it on a plate, making a depression in the center. Heat for 1 minute. Microwaves are attracted to the edges of the food rather than the center. Toast or heat buns or breads separately.

To dry herbs, spread paper towels on paper plates, put the herbs on the paper towels, and heat for 50 seconds. Allow to stand for 10 seconds and repeat for 10-second cooking-time intervals until completely dry. Discard stems and place herbs in clean, dry jars with tightly fitting lids. Store in a dark place.

To melt preserves for glazes and the foundations of dessert sauces, heat them in the jar, with the lid removed, for 5 minutes; then strain the preserves.

Disadvantages of Cooking in a Microwave Oven

ACCURATE TIMING

Microwave ovens vary in efficiency, and it is therefore important to refer to the literature that accompanies your own model. Other variations in cooking times will result from the quality of the ingredients, the starting temperature, and the shape of the food. It is as necessary to use your own judgment in assessing when the food is ready as it is in cooking by conventional means.

Remember that the food cooked in a microwave oven will continue to cook after it is removed from the oven for times ranging from a few seconds to several minutes, depending on the density of the food. It is as easy to overcook as it is to undercook foods and, as with all things, experience is the only reliable guide to absolute perfection.

TEXTURE

It is thought by some people that the texture of meat is changed and softened when cooked in the microwave oven. This is a question of personal taste, and an individual judgment must be made on the question of whether a slight alteration is justified by the greatly increased speed in cooking.

Great care must be taken in reheating bread and pastry, as the texture becomes rapidly softened.

Foods enclosed in a skin or membrane, such as potatoes, kidneys, liver, oysters, escargots, and eggs tend to "explode" in the microwave oven. There are those who claim that these foods can be cooked triumphantly with microwave energy, but I have not met with similar success in spite of repeated attempts to duplicate their cleverness. I have found that this group of foods is much better cooked by conventional means. See specific recipes for further information.

Foods do not achieve a brown, crisp crust when cooked in the microwave oven. This effect can be achieved only in the conventional oven.

All foods cook more rapidly at the edges than in the center. Soft and semisoft foods must be stirred, and solid foods must be rotated to compensate for this effect.

No metal utensils can be used in the microwave oven.

Food for a complete meal must be cooked in a sequence rather than simultaneously; that is, the meat is cooked first, then the starch (potatoes or rice), and finally the vegetables. The greater the overall volume of food in the microwave oven, the slower the cooking process.

Salt

Do not sprinkle the surface of meats with salt before cooking, as salt distorts the pattern of the microwaves and makes a tough exterior. However, salt can be added to foods cooked in a liquid. Where exceptions to this rule occur, they have been noted in specific recipes.

Covering the Pans

When a recipe calls for the ingredients to be covered, a nonmetallic lid should be used: a glass or ceramic casserole top, a plate, or a piece of waxed paper. The main purpose of covering the food is to prevent splattering in the oven. While some foods are covered to prevent them from becoming dry, the drying-out of food is less of a problem in microwave cooking than in the conventional oven, because the air surrounding the food in the microwave oven is cold and moist. In the conventional oven it is hot and dry.

Time Settings in the Microwave Oven

The recipes in this book are all cooked on the highest setting unless otherwise stated. The highest setting allows the maximum energy to cook the food. When the setting is reduced to "roast," "defrost," or other speeds, part of the microwaves are prevented from entering the oven by an "on-off" system. In the "defrost" setting, for example, the oven is in effect on for eight-tenths of a second and off for two-tenths of a second. (Different ovens vary in the "on-off" cycles.) By controlling the amount of energy, the rate of cooking is also controlled.

In passing, it is interesting to note that the highest setting is used less frequently than the lower settings. There is a great improvement in the quality of the food if it is cooked at a slightly lower speed than the maximum available.

appetizers
and soups

swiss fondue

swiss fondue

Though either Swiss or Gruyère can be used for making fondue, the imported cheese from the mountainous Gruyère region of Switzerland gives the deepest, creamiest, and richest flavor.

Yield: 8 servings

1 cup white wine
(Chablis or California white wine)
2 whole cloves garlic, peeled
¾ pound (3 cups) grated Gruyère or
Swiss cheese
3 tablespoons flour

Freshly ground black pepper
3 tablespoons kirsch
3 tablespoons butter
¼ cup heavy cream
1 teaspoon salt

Pour the wine into a 1½-quart earthenware pot, a clay pot, or a glass casserole. Add the garlic. Cook uncovered on "simmer" setting for 5 minutes. Discard the garlic cloves.

Combine the cheese, flour, and pepper and stir into the hot wine. Simmer for 3 minutes. Stir in the kirsch, butter, and cream. Simmer for 4 more minutes. Season with salt.

Serve immediately with cubes of fresh, crusty French bread and chilled white wine. Spear the bread cubes with fondue forks and swirl into the hot fondue.

Mushroom caps, quickly fried in hot butter, as well as salami, carrot sticks, and cauliflower sprigs, make delicious contrasts of taste and texture with the fondue. In Switzerland there is also a bowl of pickled onions and potatoes boiled in their jackets to eat with the fondue.

marinated steak kebabs

These appetizers are marinated in wine, cooked at the last moment, and served sizzling hot, tender, and juicy.

Yield: 6 servings

1 pound sirloin steak, weighed without the bone
½ cup red wine
2 tablespoons oil
1 tablespoon soy sauce
1 clove garlic, finely chopped
2 tablespoons cracked black pepper
2 tablespoons oil

Cut the steak into bite-size cubes and place in a bowl. Add the wine, 2 tablespoons oil, soy sauce, and garlic. Marinate the steak for 2 hours. Remove and dry on paper towels. Press the cracked pepper onto the surface of the beef.

Heat the ceramic browning plate on the highest setting for 4 minutes. Add the remaining 2 tablespoons oil. Add the steak cubes and cook for 2 minutes on each side. They should be rare in the center. Serve with toothpicks.

Note: A ceramic browning plate is supplied with some models of microwave ovens. If your oven does not have one, use a shallow Corning ⓜ skillet.

stuffed vine leaves

This is a favorite Greek recipe that is very successfully cooked in the microwave oven.

Yield: 6 servings

1 jar (16 ounces) vine leaves
1½ tablespoons olive oil
1 medium-size onion, finely chopped
¾ cup rice
1½ cups water
½ cup white raisins soaked in ½ cup water
½ cup pine nuts
2 tablespoons finely chopped parsley
½ teaspoon salt
Freshly ground black pepper
½ teaspoon cinnamon
2 medium-size tomatoes, peeled, seeded, and chopped
Water
Juice of 1 lemon

Unfold the vine leaves carefully and rinse under cold running water. Drain. Heat the olive oil in a 1-quart glass or ceramic casserole on the highest setting for 30 seconds. Add the onion and cook 1 minute. Add the rice and cook 2 minutes. Stir in the water, drained raisins, and pine nuts. Cover and cook 10 minutes. Remove and let stand for 10 minutes. Stir in the parsley, salt, pepper, cinnamon, and tomatoes.

Place approximately 1 tablespoon of the mixture on each vine leaf. Fold up the stem end to enclose the stuffing. Fold the sides to the center and roll to form a neat package. The vine leaves will hold together without any other means of securing them.

Place a layer of vine leaves in a glass baking dish. Cover with a layer of unfilled vine leaves and cover with a second layer of stuffed vine leaves. Add sufficient water to barely cover the vine leaves and add the lemon juice. Weight with a plate. Cover with waxed paper and cook for 20 minutes on the highest setting. Allow to cool for 1 hour. Drain and chill until serving time. Serve cold.

rice

Rice is cooked in the microwave oven in 10 minutes. As it can be reheated very successfully, it may be convenient for you to double the recipe and keep a supply of cooked rice in the refrigerator. To reheat, place the rice in a small casserole. Cover and cook for 1 minute.

Yield: 6 servings

2 cups boiling water	**1 tablespoon butter**
½ teaspoon salt	**1 cup long-grain rice**

Pour the water into a 1-quart glass casserole. Add the remaining ingredients. Cover and cook for 10 minutes on the highest setting. Remove from the oven and let stand for 10 more minutes.

Picture on next page: stuffed vine leaves

vichyssoise

Vichyssoise is the cold summer soup that was created in 1910 by chef Louis Diat to honor the gala opening of the roof garden at the Ritz Carlton Hotel in New York City. The soup was an instant success and is still as popular as it was in the first public unveiling of the masterpiece.

Yield: 6 servings

2 pounds potatoes (about 4 medium-size potatoes)
6 leeks or 3 yellow onions, finely chopped
6 cups chicken broth, hot
1 cup heavy cream
1 teaspoon salt
Chopped chives
Freshly ground black pepper

Peel the potatoes, cut into small pieces, and place in a 2-quart glass or ceramic casserole. Slice the white part and the lower third of the green part of the leeks. Wash in plenty of cold water to remove sand from the leeks. Add the leeks or onions to the potatoes along with the hot chicken broth. Cover and cook on the highest setting for 10 minutes, until the potatoes are very soft. Purée the soup in a blender. Add the cream and salt and chill for 4 hours before serving. Garnish with chopped chives and black pepper.

Note: Cold soups need more salt than hot soups.

watercress and potato soup

If you have never tasted this, you may be surprised to see how such simple ingredients can make such a good soup.

Yield: 4 servings

1 bunch watercress
2 tablespoons butter
1 onion, finely chopped
1 stalk celery, chopped
2 medium-size potatoes, peeled and cut into small pieces
3 cups chicken broth
1 tablespoon lemon juice
½ teaspoon salt
Freshly ground black pepper
½ cup heavy cream

Wash the watercress. Reserve ½ cup of the leaves and chop the remaining leaves and stems into small pieces. Using the highest setting throughout this recipe, heat the butter in a 2-quart glass or ceramic casserole for 20 seconds. Add the onion and celery and cook uncovered for 2 minutes. Add the watercress, potatoes, chicken broth, lemon juice, salt, and pepper. Cover and cook for 15 minutes. Purée these ingredients in the blender and return to the pan. Add the cream and heat for 2 minutes, until very hot. Add the reserved watercress leaves and serve hot or cold.

Picture on next page: watercress and potato soup

chicken soup

A splendid idea for lunch. All you need to go with it is a basketful of crusty rolls and some fruit for dessert.

Yield: 4 servings

1 2½-pound chicken, cut into serving pieces
4 cups water
1 onion or 2 leeks, chopped
2 carrots, diced
3 chicken bouillon cubes
1 cup fresh peas
2 tablespoons chopped parsley
Salt and pepper

Place the chicken in a 2-quart glass or ceramic casserole. Add 2 cups of water, the onion or leeks, and carrots. Cover and cook on the highest setting for 30 minutes.

Cool the chicken and discard the skin and bones. Cut the meat into small pieces and place to one side. Skim the fat from the surface of the broth in the casserole. Add the remaining 2 cups of water, the bouillon cubes, peas, and parsley. Cook for 2 minutes. Add the chicken pieces and season with salt and pepper. Continue cooking, uncovered, for 2 more minutes, until the soup is hot.

goulash soup

This soup has no added thickening, as the potato and the other ingredients give it body.

Yield: 6 servings

2 tablespoons butter
2 tablespoons oil
3 medium-size onions, sliced
1 clove garlic, finely chopped
2 teaspoons paprika
½ pound veal, ground
¼ pound pork, ground
4 cups stock (can be made with 4 bouillon cubes and 4 cups boiling water)
Salt and pepper
2 medium-size potatoes, sliced
3 small tomatoes, chopped
6 thin slices French bread

Heat butter and oil in a 3-quart glass or ceramic casserole on the highest setting for 20 seconds. Add onions and garlic and fry for 2 minutes. Add paprika and cook for 30 seconds. Stir in the ground meats, and cook for 2 minutes.
Gradually add the stock, and season to taste. Cover and cook on highest setting for 5 minutes. Add potato and tomato, and cook covered for 8 minutes longer, until the potatoes are soft. Toast bread in toaster or in a broiler until crisp and brown. Serve with the soup.

goulash soup

crab and corn soup

This is a soup to warm the soul of any fisherman.

Yield: 4 servings

3 tablespoons butter	½ teaspoon salt
⅓ cup flour	⅛ teaspoon pepper
2 cups milk	¼ cup table cream
2 cups cold water	Slices of tomato (optional)
1 6-ounce can crab meat	Watercress (optional)
12-ounce can whole-kernel corn	

Melt the butter in a 1½-quart glass or ceramic casserole for 30 seconds on the highest setting. Stir in flour with a wire whisk. While continuing to stir. Gradually stir in milk and water. Cook for 5 minutes or until thickened. During cooking stir twice with whisk to make a smooth sauce.

Drain crab and corn. Break crab meat into pieces, removing cartilage. Stir crab meat and corn into the sauce. Season with salt and pepper. Cover casserole and cook for 5 minutes on "simmer" setting. Remove from oven and stir in cream. Garnish with slices of tomato and watercress.

20

meats

Cooking Meats

As a general guide allow 6 minutes per pound for rare meats; 7 minutes per pound for medium meats, and 8 minutes per pound for well-done meats. Remember that all foods continue to cook after they are removed from the oven. Check the temperature of a roast after it is removed from the oven. The temperature will continue to rise 10 to 20 degrees, depending on the density of the meat. Rest small roasts 10 minutes before carving; rest larger roasts, more than 3 pounds in weight, for 15 minutes.

Do not salt the surface of meat before cooking, as salt distorts the pattern of the microwaves, slowing down the cooking and toughening the surface. Arrange foods in a circle or, as in the case of frankfurters, with a 1-inch space between each frankfurter, as microwaves are attracted to the edges of the food. Cook chicken breasts in the center of a baking dish and arrange the legs around the sides of the dish.

beef stew

Stewing beef cooks too rapidly on the highest setting of the microwave oven; all stews are much more successfully prepared at the "simmer" speed. The beef can be browned first either in a frying pan on top of the stove or on the browning plate that is supplied with the newer ovens.

Yield: 6 servings

2½ pounds boneless chuck steak
3 tablespoons oil
1 onion, finely chopped
1 clove garlic, finely chopped
2 carrots, diced
2 stalks celery, sliced

2 tablespoons flour
1½ cups beef broth
2 teaspoons tomato paste
½ teaspoon thyme
1 bay leaf

Trim the beef and cut into 1-inch cubes. Brown the cubes in hot oil and transfer to a 2-quart glass or ceramic casserole. Cook the onion, garlic, carrots, and celery in the same oil for 2 minutes. Stir in the flour and ½ cup of the beef broth. Transfer to the casserole with the beef and add the remaining broth and seasonings. Cover and cook at "simmer" setting for 50 minutes.

Cool and chill overnight; then reheat on "reheat" speed for 10 minutes. Rotate the dish and stir the stew once after 5 minutes. Discard the bay leaf before serving.

beef stewed in red wine

This is a delicious casserole meal.

Yield: 6 servings

1½ pounds boneless chuck steak, cut into 1½-inch cubes
2 tablespoons butter
1 tablespoon oil
1 large turnip, cut into 1-inch pieces
1 rutabaga, cut into 1-inch pieces
1 pound small white onions, peeled
1 pound carrots, cut into 1-inch pieces
3 tablespoons flour
1 cup beef bouillon
1 cup red wine
Dash of Worcestershire sauce
½ teaspoon peppercorns
3 bay leaves

Heat butter and oil in a 3-quart glass or ceramic casserole for 20 seconds. Brown beef, turnip, rutabaga, onions, and carrots for 4 minutes. Add flour, stir, and cook for another 2 minutes. Add bouillon, wine, Worcestershire sauce, peppercorns, and bay leaves. Cover and cook at "simmer" setting for 50 minutes. Leave overnight and reheat next day.

beef stewed in red wine

skillet supper

skillet supper

Yield: 6 servings

½ pound ground beef
3 tablespoons oil
2 onions, sliced
1 clove garlic, minced
1 small eggplant,
  cut into ½-inch cubes
1 8-ounce can tomato sauce

1 small green pepper, chopped
½ teaspoon salt
¼ teaspoon pepper
4 ounces egg noodles,
  cooked, drained
6 eggs
¼ teaspoon cayenne pepper

Place the ground beef in a 1-quart glass bowl. Cook for 2 minutes on the highest setting and drain the accumulated fat. Stir the beef with a fork and put to one side. Heat the oil in a 12-inch glass bowl for 20 seconds on the same setting. Add the onions and garlic and cook for 1 minute. Add ground beef, eggplant, tomatoes, green pepper, salt, and pepper. Cover and cook for 4 minutes. Add cooked noodles and mix thoroughly. With back of spoon make 6 hollows in meat mixture. Break an egg into each hollow. Cover tightly with a lid or plastic wrap. Cook eggs on "roast" setting for about 8 minutes or until eggs are cooked to desired doneness. Let stand, covered, for 2 minutes before serving.

macaroni cauliflower casserole

macaroni-cauliflower casserole

This is cauliflower cheese with a difference for an economical and filling meal.

Yield: 4 servings

2 tablespoons butter	1 tablespoon cooking oil
1 small onion, finely chopped	1 teaspoon salt
½ pound ground beef	4 ounces elbow macaroni
3 tablespoons catsup	(about 1 cup)
¼ cup water	2 tablespoons butter
½ teaspoon salt	2 tablespoons flour
⅛ teaspoon pepper	1¼ cups milk
1 small cauliflower,	1 egg, lightly beaten
broken into florets	1 cup cheddar cheese, grated
2 cups water	To garnish: parsley sprigs

25

Heat 2 tablespoons butter in a 1-quart glass casserole on the highest setting for 20 seconds. Add onion and ground beef and fry for 2 minutes. Drain fat and add catsup, water, salt, and pepper; cook on "reheat" setting for 5 minutes.

In a separate covered glass casserole cook cauliflower in ½ cup water for 8 minutes. Rotate dish one-quarter of a turn halfway through the cooking period. Remove cauliflower with a slotted spoon.

Bring 2 cups of water, 1 tablespoon cooking oil, and 1 teaspoon salt to a full boil in a 2-quart glass casserole on highest setting. Stir in macaroni. Recover, and cook on "defrost" setting for 10 to 12 minutes. Drain well.

Melt the remaining 2 tablespoons of butter in a glass dish on the highest setting for 20 seconds. Stir in flour with a wire whisk. Gradually stir in the milk. Cook for 3 minutes or until thick. Stir twice during cooking to give a smooth sauce. Season to taste. Remove from heat and stir in beaten egg and ½ cup of cheese.

Mix macaroni and cauliflower with the prepared sauce. Oil a 3-quart glass casserole and add ground beef mixture. Top with macaroni and cauliflower in cheese sauce. Sprinkle with remaining grated cheese. Cook on "reheat" setting for 5 minutes or until hot. Place in a preheated conventional oven at 400° F for the last 10 minutes to brown the topping. Garnish with parsley.

tagliatelle bolognese

This Italian dish is delicious from your microwave oven.

Yield: 4 to 6 servings

meat sauce

2 tablespoons butter	1 bay leaf
1 onion, finely chopped	½ cup cup beef bouillon
1 carrot, diced	½ teaspoon salt
1 stalk celery, diced	⅛ teaspoon pepper
1 clove garlic (optional), finely chopped	1 teaspoon sugar
2 strips bacon, diced	¾ pound Tagliatelle or other pasta
½ pound ground beef	⅓ cup grated Parmesan cheese
1 8-ounce can tomato sauce	

Heat butter in a 3-quart glass casserole on the highest setting for 20 seconds. Add vegetables and diced bacon. Cook for 2 minutes. Add ground beef and cook on highest setting for 7 minutes; drain. Stir in tomato sauce, bay leaf, bouillon, salt, pepper, and sugar. Cover with a glass lid and cook on "reheat" setting for 7 minutes. Taste and add more seasoning if necessary. Remove the bay leaf.

In a 3-quart covered glass casserole, bring 6 cups of water, 1 tablespoon cooking oil, and 1 teaspoon salt to a full boil on highest setting. Stir in pasta and re-cover. Cook on "defrost" setting for 14 minutes or until tender. Drain and rinse thoroughly. Turn into a hot serving dish, pour cooked meat sauce into the center, and sprinkle with Parmesan cheese.

Picture on next page: tagliatelle bolognese

butterfly leg of lamb

Ask the butcher to remove the bone from the lamb and "butterfly" it. You will then have a flattish piece of meat to serve 6 people. The meat will be cooked in less than 20 minutes.

Yield: 6 servings

1 3-pound leg of lamb, weighed after the bone is removed
1 slice bread, broken into 6 pieces
½ cup parsley
1 teaspoon rosemary
3 tablespoons butter
2 cloves garlic, finely chopped
Salt and pepper

Place the lamb, fat side down, on a microwave oven roasting rack or on top of an inverted saucer set in a glass baking dish.

Place the bread, parsley, and rosemary in a blender and blend until finely chopped. Spread the mixture on the surface of the lamb.

Heat the butter and garlic in a custard cup on the highest setting for 40 seconds. Drizzle the garlic butter over the lamb.

Cook the lamb on the highest setting for 10 minutes. Rotate the dish one-quarter of a turn and cook on "roast" setting for 8 minutes. Season with salt and pepper and leave to rest for 10 minutes before slicing.

roast lamb

roast lamb

For rare lamb cook for 8 minutes per pound. For medium lamb cook for 9 minutes per pound. For well-done lamb cook for 10 minutes per pound.

To acheive moist lamb with excellent taste, texture, and color, the roast should be cooked for the second half of the estimated time at a slower speed. If your oven does not have a "roast" setting, place a glass of hot water in the oven during the second half of the cooking time. The water will deflect some of the microwave energy and slow the cooking process.

Yield: 6 servings

1 5-pound leg of lamb with the bone	**1 teaspoon rosemary**
3 cloves garlic	**Freshly ground pepper**
3 tablespoons butter, melted	**Salt**

Trim the excess fat from the lamb. Make a series of slits in the surface of the lamb with the point of a sharp knife. Cut the garlic into slivers and insert tiny pieces of garlic into the slits. Brush the lamb with melted butter. Press the rosemary onto the surface of the lamb and season with pepper.

Place the lamb fat side down on a rack or on an inverted saucer set in a glass or ceramic baking dish. Cook on the highest setting for 20 minutes. Turn the lamb on its other side and brush with butter. Cook on "roast" setting or place a glass of hot water in the oven for 20 minutes longer (150°F) for rare lamb; 25 more minutes (160°F) for medium lamb, and 30 more minutes (170°F) for well-done lamb. Season with salt and cover with aluminum foil. Allow to stand for 15 minutes before carving. The temperature will continue to rise during this resting time.

pork chops bagatelle

pork chops bagatelle

Stacked or skewered foods can be cooked in a microwave oven if wooden hibachi skewers are used instead of metal skewers.

Yield: 4 servings

    8 pork chops
    8 slices Gruyère cheese
    4 slices ham
    2 eggs, beaten
    Bread crumbs
    ¼ cup butter

Stack in sequence and skewer 1 pork chop, 1 slice cheese, ½ slice ham, a second slice of cheese, and another pork chop. Repeat for other 3 skewers. Coat with egg and dip into bread crumbs. Heat butter in a glass baking dish on highest setting for 20 seconds. Add chops and cook on each side for 1 minute. Cover and cook on "roast" setting for 12 to 15 minutes or until pork is thoroughly cooked.

pork and orange casserole

pork and orange casserole

This dinner is both nutritious and colorful.

Yield: 4 servings

3 tablespoons oil
2 onions, finely chopped
1½ pounds lean pork, cut into 1½-inch cubes
½ cup seasoned flour
Grated rind and juice of 1 orange
11-ounce can mandarin oranges
1 cup water
1 chicken bouillon cube
1 green pepper, sliced

Heat the oil in a 2-quart glass or ceramic casserole on the highest setting for 20 seconds. Add the onions and cook for 2 minutes. Add pork coated in seasoned flour. Cook in hot fat for a few seconds to seal in juices. Toss to seal. Grate rind. Squeeze the orange. Drain the mandarin oranges. Mix the syrup from the can with the fresh juice. Combine syrup and juice with water, rind, bouillon cube, and sliced pepper in a small glass or ceramic bowl. Cook on "simmer" setting for 5 minutes. Add to pork. Cover and cook for 20 minutes on "roast" setting. Rotate dish one-quarter of a turn after 10 minutes. Add the mandarin oranges during last 5 minutes. Let stand 10 minutes before serving.

frankfurters with sauerkraut

Other meats, such as cooked pork chops, thickly sliced bacon, or a variety of sausages, including knockwurst, bratwurst, and pork sausages, can also be used to make this dish. Serve with mustard, potatoes baked in their jackets, and a mug of beer.

Yield: 4 servings

1 pound prepared sauerkraut
3 slices bacon
1 teaspoon caraway seeds
½ cup white wine
2 small boiled potatoes, grated
8 frankfurters
Freshly ground black pepper

Rinse the sauerkraut in cold water and squeeze dry. Place the bacon slices in a baking dish. Cook for 3 minutes on the highest setting, until crisp. Crumble the bacon and return it to the baking dish. Add all the remaining ingredients. Cover and cook 6 minutes. Rotate the dish a quarter of a turn after 3 minutes.

poultry

Cooking Poultry

Chicken, turkey, and other poultry are moist and tender when they are cooked in the microwave oven. To obtain the best results, all poultry that is to be roasted should be trussed with string before cooking. The tips of the wings and the lower parts of the legs can be wrapped loosely with lightweight aluminum foil to prevent them from becoming overcooked. Make sure the foil does not touch the oven walls or there will be "arcing" of the microwaves. Do not salt the skin of poultry before cooking, because salt deflects the pattern of the microwaves and slows down the cooking. However, the cavity of chickens and other birds may be salted.

All poultry to be roasted is cooked breast side down on the highest setting for the first half of the cooking time. The bird is then turned over onto its back and cooked for the remaining time, uncovered, on "roast" setting.

Check the temperature of the cooked poultry immediately after it is taken from the oven. The thermometer should read 175° F. The temperature will rise 20 degrees as the bird stands. Let it rest for 15 minutes after cooking. During this time the cooking will be completed as a result of the transference of its own internal heat.

chicken with mandarins

chicken with mandarins

Poultry should be completely thawed before cooking. Use a microwave rack.

Yield: 4 to 6 servings

1 5-pound roasting chicken	2 tablespoons butter, melted
2 cups orange juice	1 tablespoon flour
2 tablespoons orange rind	Orange or mandarin segments
1/3 cup brown sugar	for garnish

Combine orange juice, orange rind, sugar, and melted butter. Place chicken in glass baking dish. Sprinkle body cavity with salt and pepper. Truss the chicken with string. Place chicken, breast side down, on microwave roasting rack in a 2-quart glass baking dish. Pour juice mixture over the chicken. Cook on highest setting for 18 minutes. Baste every 15 minutes with pan juices. Turn breast side up and cook on "roast" setting for 18 minutes. Transfer chicken to a hot serving plate and cover with foil for 5 to 10 minutes before serving.

Mix flour with 2 tablespoons cold water and stir into pan drippings with a wire whisk. Bring to a boil on highest setting and cook for 2 minutes or until the sauce has thickened. Stir once after 1 minute. Garnish chicken with orange or mandarin segments and serve with rice or oven-fried potatoes. Serve the sauce separately.

chicken pie

To blend flavors, refrigerate this prior to serving.

Yield: 6 servings

3-pound chicken	2 cups water	10-ounce package frozen peas
1 teaspoon salt	1/4 cup butter	3 tablespoons shortening
1/4 teaspoon pepper	3 1/2 cups flour	1 small egg, lightly beaten
1 bay leaf	5 tablespoons milk	Slices of cucumber for garnish

Wash chicken; pat dry. Place in a 3-quart glass casserole. Add salt, pepper, bay leaf, and 2 cups of water. Cover and cook on highest setting for 15 minutes. Turn chicken and cook on "simmer" setting for 40 minutes or until chicken is tender. Drain chicken, reserve stock, and cool.

Melt 1/4 cup butter in a medium glass bowl on highest setting for 20 seconds. Add 1/2 cup flour and blend thoroughly. Cook for 2 minutes, stirring twice.

Use 2 cups of broth. Gradually stir into the flour mixture. Heat on highest setting for 2 to 3 minutes, until boiling.

Remove chicken meat from bones and cut up. Mix with sauce and stir in peas. Season with salt and pepper.

Sift rest of flour and a pinch of salt into a mixing bowl. Add remaining margarine and shortening. Cut with two knives or a pastry blender until mixture resembles cornmeal. Add just enough cold water to make a stiff dough. Roll out 2/3 of dough and line an 8-inch baking dish.

Spoon filling into dish. Roll out rest of dough to make a lid for the pie. Put in place. Trim and decorate edge. Reroll trimmings and cut out shapes to decorate top of pie. Brush with beaten egg and bake on "roast" setting for 9 minutes. Transfer to preheated conventional oven at 450°F and bake 10 to 15 minutes or until golden brown.

roast turkey with two sauces

roast turkey with two sauces

These sauces give turkey an unusual and delicious accent.

Yield: 10 servings

1 10-pound turkey	¼ cup Madeira wine
1 teaspoon salt	Oil for basting
½ teaspoon pepper	

Season inside of turkey. Marinate the turkey liver in wine for 15 minutes and return to cavity of bird with 2 tablespoons of the wine. Truss with string. Cook turkey breast side down on microwave roasting rack. Cook on highest setting for 40 minutes, turning turkey once during cooking time. Continue cooking on "roast" setting for 40 minutes, turning turkey once. Serve with sauces.

aphrodisiac sauce

Yield: Sauce for 10

12 small white onions, chopped or thinly sliced
½ cup olive oil
1 tablespoon cinnamon
½ pound raisins (1½ cups)
1½ cups giblet broth (or chicken bouillon)
½ 6-ounce can tomato paste

Heat oil on highest setting for 2 minutes. Carefully add onions, and cook for 5 minutes. Stir at least twice during cooking period. When soft, add the cinnamon, raisins, and broth. Add enough tomato paste to give a sharp taste. Cook on "simmer" setting until well-heated.

metoufe sauce

Yield: Sauce for 10

6 medium-size onions, finely chopped
6 medium-size tomatoes, finely chopped
1 tablespoon parsley, finely chopped
½ cup olive oil
2 tablespoons crushed pimientos

Combine all ingredients, mix thoroughly, and serve.

bread sauce

This sauce is delicious when served with roast poultry.

Yield: 4 servings

1¼ cups milk	¼ teaspoon pepper
1 tablespoon finely grated onion	⅛ teaspoon nutmeg
3 whole cloves	1 tablespoon melted butter
½ teaspoon salt	¾ cup fresh white bread crumbs

Pour milk into a small glass bowl. Add onions and cloves. Bring to a boil on highest setting. Reduce heat to "simmer" setting and cook for 2 minutes. Remove cloves. Season with salt and pepper. Add nutmeg. Add butter and bread crumbs to the milk and blend well. On "simmer" setting, cook until hot.

spatchcock turkey

Turkey legs are on sale at various times of the year. They offer excellent food value and a low-cost meal.

Yield: 4 servings

> 2 turkey legs and thighs, cut at joint into serving pieces
> 2 teaspoons poultry seasoning
> 1 teaspoon salt
> 2 lemons, thinly sliced
> ¼ cup chutney
> 1 tablespoon catsup
> 1 lemon, juiced
> ¼ cup soft brown sugar
> 4 whole fresh tomatoes
> 4 baked or sautéed potatoes

Rub poultry seasoning and salt into turkey. Cover each with lemon slices. In a small glass bowl or casserole combine chutney, catsup, lemon juice, and sugar. On "simmer" setting, heat 1 or 2 minutes, until bubbling. Spoon over turkey joints and cook uncovered on "roast" setting for 20 minutes. Serve with baked tomatoes and baked or sautéed potatoes. Tomato skins must be pierced in several places before cooking in microwave oven. Garnish with lemon slices and parsley.

turkey and cheese cauliflower

It is much easier to remove cooked turkey from the bone while it is still warm—if turkey has cooled, place in colander over hot water until the skin and turkey flesh have softened.

Yield: 4 servings

> 1 medium-size cauliflower, cut in large florets
> Oil and vinegar dressing (mix ⅛ cup oil and ⅛ cup vinegar)
> ½ cup mayonnaise
> ¼ cup whipping cream
> 1 cup cooked turkey, chopped
> Salt and pepper
> ¼ cup grated cheddar cheese

Cook cauliflower. Drain and sprinkle with oil and vinegar dressing. Mix mayonnaise with cream. Add salt and pepper to taste. Add turkey and cauliflower in glass or ceramic bowl; spoon over turkey sauce. Sprinkle with cheese.

Cook for 4 minutes on highest setting. Rotate dish one-quarter turn after 2 minutes. The cheese will not brown in the microwave oven unless you have one of the newer models with the browning element.

spatchcock turkey

seafood

striped bass

All fish are excellent when they are cooked in the microwave oven. In this recipe the fish is topped with fresh vegetables and flavored with a whisper of lemon butter. If you are using frozen fish, allow 10 minutes for it to defrost in your microwave oven.

Yield: 2 servings

1 pound striped bass, cleaned and bones removed
2 scallions, finely chopped
1 small tomato, peeled, seeded, and chopped

½ cup cucumber, diced
¼ teaspoon tarragon or 1 tablespoon chopped parsley
2 tablespoons butter
1 tablespoon lemon juice

Place the bass on a piece of waxed paper large enough to enclose it completely. Top the fish with all the remaining ingredients. Fold the long sides of the paper over the fish and tuck the edges beneath, forming a tidy package. Place on inverted plates and cook for 6 minutes on the highest setting. Rotate the fish one-quarter of a turn after 3 minutes.

braised halibut in cream and white wine

Other firm-textured fish, such as cod, salmon, bass, trout, or swordfish, can also be used for making this dish.

Yield: 6 servings

3 pounds halibut
4 scallions, finely chopped
2 carrots, thinly sliced
2 stalks celery, thinly sliced
½ teaspoon thyme
Grated rind of 1 lemon

2 tablespoons butter
½ cup cream
½ cup white wine
1½ tablespoons flour
Salt and pepper
2 tablespoons freshly chopped parsley

Place the fish in a 10-inch glass or ceramic baking dish. Arrange the vegetables around the sides of the dish. Sprinkle the fish with thyme and grated lemon rind. Dot with 1 tablespoon of the butter. Pour in the cream and wine. Cover with waxed paper and cook on "roast" setting for 12 minutes. Rotate the dish one-quarter of a turn after 6 minutes. Transfer the fish to a hot platter and season with salt and pepper. Allow to stand for 5 minutes. It should flake easily, indicating it is completely cooked.

Heat the remaining 1 tablespoon of butter in a 6-cup glass measuring cup on the highest setting for 20 seconds and then stir into the vegetables and liquid in the baking dish. Cook for 5 minutes on the same setting. Spoon the sauce over the fish and garnish with parsley.

fillets of sole with vegetables

fillets of sole with vegetables

Fish is done when it is white and opaque. Separate the flakes near the center with a fork to test that it is fully cooked.

Yield: 2 servings

2 fillets of sole (about 1 pound)
¾ cup heavy cream
1 stalk celery, thinly sliced
1 scallion, thinly sliced
2 carrots, thinly sliced
½ teaspoon salt
1 tablespoon butter

Melt the 1 tablespoon of butter in a medium baking dish for 20 seconds on the highest setting. Add vegetable slices and salt. Cook for 2 minutes. While stirring rapidly, add the cream. Cook for 3 minutes. Add in the sole and cook 3 minutes. Remove fillets of sole and set on serving plate. Cook sauce 1 additional minute. Take out of oven. Pour sauce over slices of sole.

fillets of sole with tomatoes

The wine used for poaching the sole becomes a delicious sauce enriched with cream.

Yield: 8 servings

3 pounds fillets of sole
¼ pound butter
1 large onion, finely chopped
3 scallions
3 sprigs parsley
½ cup chopped watercress
2 large tomatoes, peeled, seeded, and chopped
½ teaspoon tarragon
½ teaspoon salt
⅛ teaspoon pepper
1 cup dry white wine
1 egg yolk, beaten
¾ cup heavy cream
1 tablespoon lemon juice

fillets of sole with tomatoes

In a large glass baking dish add butter, onion, scallions, watercress, tomatoes, and tarragon. Add the sole to the dish. Add salt, pepper, and wine. Cover and cook on highest setting for 12 minutes. Let stand, covered, for 5 minutes. Remove the fillets and keep them warm. Continue to cook the sauce until the volume is reduced by one-third. Remove from microwave oven and rapidly stir in the egg yolk and the cream. Taste and adjust seasoning as desired. Add lemon juice. Return the fillets to the cooking dish and spoon the sauce over them. Broil in a conventional broiler on low heat for 5 minutes to brown.

seafood rissoto

haddock with tomato sauce

This quickly prepared meal must be made with the freshest of fish and the ripest of summer tomatoes. If frozen fish and canned tomatoes are used, it may look similar, but it will be a mere hint of its potential delight.

Yield: 4 servings

2 pounds haddock
2 tablespoons butter

tomato sauce

4 medium-size tomatoes,
**   cut into wedges**
1 onion, finely chopped
2 tablespoons white vermouth
1 tablespoon olive oil

1 teaspoon flour
2 teaspoons tomato paste
½ teaspoon thyme
½ teaspoon basil
Salt and pepper

Dot the haddock with butter. Wrap it in waxed paper. Place it in a 10-inch glass or ceramic baking dish and cook on the highest setting for 6 minutes. Rotate the dish one-quarter of a turn after 3 minutes.

To prepare the sauce, place all the ingredients in a glass or ceramic casserole. Cover and cook on the highest setting for 8 minutes. Purée the sauce in a blender and strain to remove the tomato skins and seeds. Reheat the sauce, uncovered, for 3 minutes and serve with the fish.

seafood rissoto

Yield: 4 servings

2 cups uncooked rice
1 small onion, chopped
¼ cup butter
½ pound medium shrimp
¼ pound mushrooms
1 stalk celery, chopped
1 red pepper, sliced
1 package frozen green peas
¼ teaspoon saffron

2 tablespoons finely chopped parsley
¼ cup grated Parmesan cheese
2 small onions, sliced
½ stalk celery
1 clove garlic
1 cup white wine
½ teaspoon salt
¼ teaspoon pepper

Peel and devein shrimp. Put stock ingredients plus shrimp peels and 2½ cups water in a 1½-quart glass or ceramic casserole. Cook at highest setting for 5 minutes. Strain.

Melt butter in a 2½-quart casserole for 20 seconds. Add onion and cook for 2 minutes, until transparent. Add rice and stir well. Pour in strained stock. Cook for 12 minutes. Rotate the dish one-quarter turn every 2 minutes. Add celery, red pepper, thawed peas, mushrooms, shrimp, and ground saffron. Cover casserole and cook 6 minutes on highest setting, until shrimp are pink. Stir mixture and rotate the dish one-quarter of a turn after 3 minutes. Before serving, sprinkle with parsley and grated Parmesan cheese.

seafood quiche lorraine

seafood quiche lorraine

Use the lowest setting for this custard dish.

Yield: 6 servings

pastry

1¼ cups flour
6 tablespoons butter
3 tablespoons cold water
3 tablespoons light cream

cheese filling

3 eggs
1¼ cups grated Gruyère cheese
¼ cup grated Parmesan cheese
¾ cup milk
½ cup light cream
¼ teaspoon paprika or white pepper
⅛ teaspoon nutmeg
½ teaspoon salt
For shellfish choose among: 4 ounces shrimp, crab, or lobster

pastry

Sift flour into a bowl. Cut in butter with a knife or pastry blender until mixture looks mealy. Make a hole in the center and pour the water and cream into it. Work the pastry with a spoon until it can be formed into a ball. Chill thoroughly. Roll out to fit an 8- or 9-inch glass pie plate. Flute edge; prick bottom and sides of crust with fork. Cook on "roast" setting for 7 minutes.

cheese and seafood filling

Beat the eggs. Add cheeses, milk, cream, seasonings, and spices. Arrange the shellfish, cleaned and shelled, in the pie shell. Pour the cream mixture into the pie shell and cook on "defrost" setting for 30 to 35 minutes or until a knife inserted in the center comes out clean. Let quiche stand 5 minutes before serving.

fish bonne femme in crepes

fish bonne femme in crepes

Although this recipe involves several steps, the total time is less than 1 hour for a delectable main dish.

Yield: 4 servings

batter

>½ cup flour
>Pinch salt
>1 egg
>5 tablespoons milk

filling

>1 pound white fish (sole, haddock, etc.) fillets
>¼ cup butter
>Salt and pepper
>2 tablespoons water
>¼ cup white wine
>½ pound mushrooms
>1 tablespoon onion, finely chopped

sauce

>3 tablespoons butter
>4 tablespoons flour
>1¼ cups milk

garnish

>Pastry crescents

Combine batter ingredients and beat to blend. Make 8 very thin crepes in the usual way. Heat half the butter in a 2-quart glass or ceramic casserole on the highest setting for 20 seconds. Add fish and cook each side for 1 minute. Sprinkle with salt and pepper, then pour the water and wine into the casserole. Cover with waxed paper and cook for 6 minutes on "simmer" setting until the fish flakes easily. While fish is cooking, slice mushrooms. Remove fish from oven and keep it warm. Heat remainder of butter in a medium glass bowl on the highest setting for 20 seconds. Stir in mushrooms and onion and cook for 2 minutes. Pour onto center of a heated serving dish and keep it warm. Fold 2 sides of each crepe into the middle to form cone shapes. Remove fish from the liquid (reserve this for sauce) and place a piece of fish in each crepe. Fold over to form a roll. Place the rolls on top of the mushroom mixture. Keep warm.

For the sauce: Melt butter in a small pan on conventional burner; stir in flour. Cook slowly to brown; gradually add milk and cook, stirring constantly, until thick. Add liquid from the fish and extra seasoning to taste, if necessary. Pour over rewarmed crepes and garnish with crescents of cooked pie pastry. (This is a useful way of using leftover pastry. The crescent can be stored in a tight container and reheated before using as a garnish.)

vegetables

Cooking Vegetables

All vegetables are cooked in covered dishes, in freezer cartons, or in plastic pouches. All are rotated one-quarter of a turn halfway through the cooking period. Salt can be added to vegetables if they are cooked in water. If they are cooked in cartons, add salt after the cooking is completed. All fresh vegetables are cooked in one-third to one-half of the conventional cooking time. Canned vegetables are cooked in the liquid in which they are canned and need only be reheated. A 1-pound can of vegetables is hot in 3 minutes. Transfer the vegetables to a 1-quart glass or ceramic casserole for reheating.

To cook vegetables frozen in cartons, remove the outer wrappings or the dye may stain the bottom of the oven. Open the carton at one end. Place icy side up and allow roughly 5 minutes cooking time on the highest setting. Err on the side of undercooking rather than overcooking, because more time can always be added, but overcooked vegetables are one of life's few avoidable disasters. Remember, too, that the vegetables continue to cook for a minute or two after they are removed from the oven.

Many frozen vegetables that are prepared in butter and packed in pouches have recommended times for microwave oven cooking printed on the box. All these times can be trusted. Cut a slit in the pouch before cooking, as the steam pressure may build so greatly within the package as to cause it to burst.

Most satisfactory results are obtained when cooking one pound or less of a vegetable. Larger quantities require a longer cooking time and are more successfully cooked on top of the stove.

asparagus with white sauce

asparagus and cottage cheese salad

This salad, made when the first tender asparagus appears in the springtime, can be served alone or with rolled slices of boiled Virginia ham.

Yield: 6 servings

1½ pounds thin asparagus spears
½ teaspoon salt
Freshly ground black pepper
2 tablespoons lemon juice
6 tablespoons olive oil

1 pound cottage cheese
1 cup sour cream
3 tablespoons chopped chives
Pimiento strips

Wash the asparagus in plenty of cold water to remove any sand. Cut the spears into uniform lengths. Peel the lower third of each spear with a potato peeler. Arrange in a 10-inch glass or ceramic flat baking dish with the tips in the center of the dish. Sprinkle with salt and add cold water to cover. Cook, covered, on the highest setting until the water reaches the boiling point. Rotate the dish one-quarter of a turn and cook for 3 more minutes. Taste a spear to be sure it is tender but slightly crisp. Drain and rinse immediately but briefly under cold running water. Return the asparagus to the baking dish.

Combine the salt, pepper, lemon juice, and oil, and pour over the warm asparagus. Let stand for 5 minutes and drain off the dressing.

Arrange the asparagus on a flat serving plate with the tips pointing to the edge of the plate. Combine the cottage cheese and sour cream and place in the center of the dish. Sprinkle with chopped chives and garnish with pimiento strips.

asparagus with white sauce

When asparagus is in season, it can be served in many delectable ways. This method is beautiful with roast chicken or ham.

Yield: 6 servings

2 pounds uniform-size fresh asparagus spears
½ cup cold water

1 tablespoon lemon juice
1 teaspoon salt
1 tablespoon butter

white sauce

2 tablespoons butter
2 tablespoons flour
¾ cup milk
¾ cup light cream

⅛ teaspoon nutmeg
Salt and pepper
2 hard-boiled eggs

Trim the asparagus (see recipe for Asparagus and Cottage Cheese Salad) and place in a baking dish. Add the water, lemon juice, and salt. Cover with waxed paper and cook on the highest setting for 6 minutes. Drain and immediately rinse under cold running water. Place on a serving dish, dot with butter, and keep the asparagus warm while preparing the sauce.

Heat the butter in a 4-cup measuring glass for 30 seconds on the highest setting. Stir in the flour, milk, cream, nutmeg, salt, and pepper, and cook for 3 minutes. Stir with a wire whisk twice to ensure a smooth sauce. Reserve 1 egg yolk. Chop the remaining yolk and whites and add to the hot sauce. Place the sauce in a sauce boat and sprinkle with the remaining chopped egg yolk. Reheat the asparagus for 1½ minutes just before serving with the sauce.

green peas bonne femme